Effective Habits of Successful People

this book are for clarifying purposes only and are owned by the owners themselves, not affiliated with this document.

TABLE OF CONTENTS

Description 8

Introduction 10

Chapter 1 11

Everything You Need to Know About Success 11

   How are we going to define success? 12

   What is the most motivating thing for you to achieve success? 12

   What can you do to enhance your sense of motivation to achieve success? 13

      Challenge yourself. 13

      Stay curious. 14

      Take control. 14

      Don't fear competition. 14

   How to Develop a Success Mindset 14

   What can you do to build an attitude of growth? 15

   The Keys to Success 15

Chapter 2 17

Personal Traits of Successful People 17

   Conscientious 17

   Capable of adaptation 17

   Intelligence 18

   Strong Mental Power 18

   Successful people Seek assistance 19

   Strong WillPOwer 19

   Courage 20

   Want to learn 20

   Competitors 21

   Ambiguity acceptance 22

Chapter 3 23

Effective habits to move towards the path of success 23

    Live with a purpose. 23

    Identify your desires..24

    Make a list of your objectives 24

    Stick to the undertakings. 25

    Be educated...25

    Manage your finances. 26

    Manage your time..27

    Enjoy the moment now. 27

    Don't equate your own life with the lives of others. 28

    Count your blessings. 28

    Look after your health...28

    Track incentives...29

    Encircle yourself with optimistic people. 30

    Know how experts are competent in transforming your life 30

    Immediate Achievement...31

Chapter 4 33

Effective Habits of Successful People 33

    They start the day in the morning..................................33

    Meditation 33

    People who excel are enduring......................................34

    Productive people are trusting in themselves................34

    Focused Thinking 34

    Good people believe high. 34

    Committed. 35

    Successful people generously contribute. 35

    It's goal-oriented 35

Regular workout 35

They are powered by tests 37

network with other people 37

Successful people have huge willpower. 37

People who excel have courage. 38

Action-oriented 38

Take enough sleep 38

Don't depend on a single revenue source 39

They avoid the waste of time...39

Efficient individuals are hopeful.......................................39

Successful individuals are flexible. 40

Productive people are mindful of their "why." 40

keep track of daily tasks 40

Continue the day with small significant tasks 40

They are conscious of health 41

They treat challenges as gifts...41

They accept defeat and restart 42

stick to routine...42

pay attention to information 42

Are Honest...42

Self-disciplined..43

Exercise self-control 44

Always looking for a solution 44

Conclusion 45

DESCRIPTION

What is success? How can you excel in life?

Some people envision money when they think about success; others want power; some just want to have a positive effect on the planet. All of these are entirely true; in reality, success is a term that means various things to different people. And no matter what progress you have, it's almost likely it won't come quickly.

There is no even one way, and an effective habit leads to success. What works for you might not work for another person. There may be no ideal mix of ingredients and habits which you can adopt to ensure success, but there are some necessary habits; if you select, it will boost your chances of success in life, marriage, work, or anything that is important to you. Whatever the era, where you live or what your career aspirations are, you are definitely going to be happy and productive with your ultimate goals in life.

Success means more than just getting money and making your mark. It means to pursue your desires, to live consciously, and to enjoy the moment. Nonetheless, there are various guides and books available related to success and effective habits because success is personal and unique to each person; therefore, it is imperative to understand how you can achieve success by following the effective habits of successful people.

The advice mentioned in this book helps you to achieve success in your daily life. Therefore it is always futile to read the ebook and learn something new. To meet the aim the ebook outlines the key points,

- Everything You Need to Know About Success
- How are we going to define success?
- What is the most motivating thing for you to achieve success?
- How to Develop a Success Mindset
- The Keys to Success
- Personal Traits of Successful People
- Effective habits to move towards the path of success
- Effective Habits of Successful People

INTRODUCTION

We seem to want to achieve success quickly in this modern world. It's a matter of instant gratification, from weight loss to internet speed to a reaction to your most recent email or text. This also covers the career field, where people tend to make money and become successful ASAPs. Verily, there's no secret hack to make you succeed overnight. However, you can add

specific habits measures to help you streamline your journey to success.

From you, success starts.

Everything you do today is a product of your attitude, inspiration, and behaviors. Therefore, if you adopt a particular set of habits in life, you can succeed. In life, success is what you consider it to be. Perhaps you want to decide whether to gain financial independence or a flexible job schedule. Some people may want to see the globe, and others only want to do what they do. If you succeed, you don't necessarily have to be rich or receive awards; real success is what you achieve yourself.

- What would it look like if you had to design your perfect day?
- Sit on a bench next to a lake and write your memoirs?
- Imagine you a Mountain and breathe that deep and big breath once you reach the top?
- Or maybe you just want to play with your children for a whole day?

You will personally know why you want to learn how to succeed in life. Your partner, parents, and friends can have a definition of success for themselves. Most people are concerned with how to succeed, and they want to know what changes and habits they can add in their life, which matters for success. We may look back on our lives, saddened by our lack of influence on the planet without any success. To aspire for a higher purpose is what keeps us fighting for survival and development. While you may not be an international star, your life will still influence others. The goal of success allows you to lead a more purposeful life by pushing you to conquer challenges, work a little harder, and find happiness. The truth is, you possibly would never win.

On the other side, learning how to succeed was never harder. In the world, there were never more millionaires than now. The simple formula to achieve success is just to choose the right and productive habits and adopt them successfully.

CHAPTER 1
EVERYTHING YOU NEED TO KNOW ABOUT SUCCESS

HOW ARE WE GOING TO DEFINE SUCCESS?

There are many different life-growth approaches, but the best approach will depend on your concept of growth and success. Some people think if he/she performs well or earns a high salary, it is a success. Some consider professional achievements as a success; it leaves out many other critical areas of life. Family, personal ties, academics, and athletics are only some fields for success. Your definition of success may vary, but many people can define it as fulfilled, happy, safe, healthy, and loved. It is the opportunity to accomplish your goals in life, regardless of your goals.

WHAT IS THE MOST MOTIVATING THING FOR YOU TO ACHIEVE SUCCESS?

Do you agree that the prospect of future rewards keeps you working for your goals, or do you feel inspired by personal, intrinsic motivators? Although external rewards like money, prizes and recognition can be helpful, many think that they are more likely to do things at a small level, but if you want to do something out of your will, or want to do as it is valuable or because you like the results of your work, you are motivated by intrinsic motives. Research has shown that while incentives can boost efficiency, they fail to predict performance and improve quality. Although external influences often inspire people, internal motivators attract people and prevent people from sustaining these new behaviors.

What Can You Do to Enhance Your Sense of Motivation to Achieve Success?

Challenge Yourself.

Achieving a feasible but not necessarily simple objective is an excellent way to motivate people to succeed. Challenges can keep you involved, strengthen your self-evaluation, and provide you feedback on how you can develop. Choosing a task that is quite difficult will help you get started — it feels exciting!

STAY CURIOUS.

Look for things you are interested in and want to know more about.

TAKE CONTROL

Take control. If you feel like you have no real control over the outcome, it can be difficult to stay emotionally motivated to achieve a goal. Find ways to play an active role.

DON'T FEAR COMPETITION.

Many may strive to accomplish the same goals as you, so you shouldn't give up. Don't equate anyone else's success or path. You should look for inspiration and encouragement for others, but note that we all have different ways.

So

What can you do to increase your chances of success?

The one and most important thing to make yourself is to change your mindset. Mindset refers to your thinking pattern.

HOW TO DEVELOP A SUCCESS MINDSET

Two fundamental behaviors affect how people think about themselves and their skills. Those with a set outlook assume that such qualities as intellect are stagnant and unchangeable. Those with a fixed mentality believe that success is not a product of hard work – it is only the result of natural talents. Since they think that people are born with or without gifts, they appear to give up more easily when facing a challenge. They stop when things aren't easy because they believe they lack the innate ability to excel.

On the other hand, growing people feel that they can change, grow, and learn by effort. Many who think they will change would most definitely thrive. They look at opportunities to develop their skills and start striving for success, while times are tough.

WHAT CAN YOU DO TO BUILD AN ATTITUDE OF GROWTH?

- **Believe your efforts are essential.** Instead of worrying about your skills set or stuck, people who are with growing thinking assume that commitment and hard work will lead to successful growth.
- **Learn new abilities.** If you face a challenge, you are looking for ways to develop the knowledge and skills to be successful.
- **View failures as experiences of learning.** People with a sense of development may not accept that failure represents their ability. Rather, they find it to be a reliable source of information to gain and grow.

THE KEYS TO SUCCESS

The keys to success in changing your life always remain the same. You can summarize them,

1. Decide just what you would like to achieve and where you would like to go.

2. Set a deadline and prepare for it. (Remember, a goal is only a deadline dream.)

3. Take action on your plan; do something to move towards your goal every day.

4. Make sure you stay in mind until you excel that you will never give up.

This formula is very useful for achieving success and worked for nearly all of us. This will take the most you can offer and build the best qualities. You must adapt and mature into an outstanding individual to establish and achieve these keys to personal achievement.

Everybody needs the success of themselves and the secret to that. Everybody deserves a happy, safe life, fulfilling work, a career, and financial freedom. Everybody wants to make a difference in the world, to be successful, and to have a positive effect on the people around him. We all want to do something different with our life and career. I've also noticed that the secrets to success are a collective experience, a simple insight that can transform your life in the right place at the right moment.I've also found that accepting big truths and realities lead to success.

CHAPTER 2
PERSONAL TRAITS OF SUCCESSFUL PEOPLE

Psychologists have tried for a long time to relate certain attributes or personality traits to success. A basic test that is frequently used by companies to screen work candidates is the Myers-Briggs Style Indicator (MBTI). However, the analysis also does not indicate that the MBTI represents success efficiency. According to more recent studies, there are certain effective characteristics of individual people that are continuously linked to success. Many personal characteristics can play a role in the way people work and think about success. Furthermore, they note that these characteristics are must be optimized to achieve success. If you want to learn how to live successfully, consider what you can do to nurture these key features:

CONSCIENTIOUS

Conscientious people take into account the effect of their decisions. They also think about how others react and feel. This functionality can be nurtured by:

- Considering the consequences of actions
- Discussing the experiences of others

CAPABLE OF ADAPTATION

Besides being able to accept ambiguity, success often depends on the ability to adapt to change quickly. You will promote this modification capability by:

- Refocusing difficult situations to see them as opportunities to learn and grow instead of just obstacles to living through
- Be open to change; look back to see how to deal with arrangements or circumstances

INTELLIGENCE

Overall, intelligence has long been considered a contributing factor to achievement in various life fields, but some researchers believe that emotional intelligence can potentially matter much more. Emotional awareness relates to the capacity to perceive, interpret, and solve. Emotionally intelligent people can understand not only their own emotions but also others. The emotionally smart, successful people not only look out for their own feelings but also concentrate on recognizing what others know and what their emotions are. Successful people are able to manage their feelings effectively. Step back and try to look impartially at things. Avoid bottling with their beliefs or repressing them, and look for healthy and suitable ways to deal with the failure. They also listen to others. This not only involves attention to what you hear but also paying note of nonverbal signals and body language.

STRONG MENTAL POWER

Mental toughness refers to continuing and even trying to cope with obstacles. Successful People with strong mental strength take challenges as opportunities. They also believe they have the power to manage their life, be confident that they will excel and dedicate to finish what they started. Successful people with adequate mental strength believe in self. Cut down negative self-talk and seek ways to remain positive and autonomous. They always keep trying. Even if things seem impossible or retrograde, focus on developing their skills and keep the soldiers on track. One of the critical behaviors of productive people is often to view reversals or failures as chances to improve. Mentally healthy people realize that they must first set realistic goals in order to achieve them. Such goals are not always easy to make, but it can help them to step forward and conquer challenges by getting something to aim for.

SUCCESSFUL PEOPLE SEEK ASSISTANCE

It can be challenging to do it yourself, but with a good support network, it can be more straightforward. When times get rough, coaches, friends, peers, and family can inspire you and can also help and assist you to boost your chances of success.

STRONG WILLPOWER

It is recognized that highly intelligent and successful people are the most productive in life and eventually shared certain main traits, including perseverance and stamina. These characteristics tend to be part of the overall personality of an individual, but they can also be improved. Delayed happiness, determination with challenges, and waiting for the results of the hard work will also be the path to progress in their life. People with strong willpower avoid distraction. For example, distracting yourself during moments of weakness can be an excellent way to avoid temptation if you try to lose weight, but have difficulties staying away from your favorite snacks. Everyone can build willpower, but it takes time and effort. Start by achieving specific goals, such as avoiding succulent snacks. As you develop your capacity to use your will power to accomplish such small targets, you may also find your willingness to work towards much larger goals more reliable.

COURAGE.

The most successful people in the world often show great courage. They are prepared to take risks, even in the face of possible failure. Research suggests that brave people use positive emotions to overcome fear. You can increase your risk tolerance by:

- Focus on positive feelings and causes of negative emotions
- A compromise between risk and traditional meaning, caution, and pragmatism, depending on the situation, may also pay off.

WANT TO LEARN

People who succeed tend to be curious about their world. They always look forward to learning more, including new skills and knowledge. They can foster their sense of curiosity through: Relate things to their interests: For instance, if you find tedious, find a more effective way to categorize the details that you want as an organizer and play with your strengths. They always want to know and learn new things.

COMPETITORS

Successful people use rivalry to inspire but resist envy. They can foster a healthy competitive environment by:

- focus on their improvements; pay attention to their own progress rather than worry about the best.
- Be happy when others are successful

Some features can be more suitable than others. However, no specific feature can guarantee success, and nobody can fail because of some particular feature.

Ambiguity Acceptance

Life is full of not always clear situations. Individuals with tremendous potential for achievement best embrace this uncertainty. We are able to adapt instead of being stiff and inflexible when the unforeseen happens. Uncertainty should be accepted by:

- Challenge your viewpoints and consider other than your own thoughts and ideas
- Not afraid of the unknown
- Be ready to change
- Diversity assessment

Chapter 3
Effective habits to move towards the path of success

Regardless of how old, where you work, or what your career aspirations are, it's usually a happy and productive end to your life. Success means more than just getting money and leaving a mark. This means pursuing the interests, living consciously, and loving the moment. Here in this section, we are going to discuss how successful people move towards the path of success.

Live with a purpose.

Successful people pay attention to their actions in order to fulfill their dreams and be the person they want to be. If you want to become successful, ask yourself, "Is it what I want to achieve? Is that I am at the right place where I achieve success? When you're constantly lonely, dreaming of the future, or the past, counting the minutes before the day comes to an end, it's presumably because you feel unconnected. Successful people enjoy their money. Enjoy their life. If you want to be successful, try spending your free time doing things you like, not wasting time. For example, you should not spend your weekends watching television or spend time with your loved ones and new friends in your hobbies. Measure your productivity by commitment, not performance. Not all in the modern sense should be successful, but behaviors should be desirable and pleasant. Keep in mind that wasting time doing nothing and being lazy one day a week is good. In fact, this can help with your imagination and consciousness. Strive for a compromise between the things that you want to do, and just "doing."

IDENTIFY YOUR DESIRES.

If you want to be successful, describe what achievement means to you before you can excel. It can take years to realize what you want to do with your life, and it can help you to identify your passions, interests, and values and give meaning to your life. If you find these items difficult to recognize, ask a friend or family member to support you. Tell yourself these questions:

- What would you like to be your legacy?
- What do you like about why people remember you?
- How do you want the world to become a safer place?
- What are some of your favorite subjects? Think of subjects you enjoyed studying in school, for example. Ask yourself why you liked them.
- You may have loved musical theatre, for sure. Think: was it because you enjoyed the music or because you enjoyed striving toward a shared purpose for a large group?

MAKE A LIST OF YOUR OBJECTIVES

If you want to achieve long term success, make a habit of preparing a list of objectives and what you can do to achieve them. Be careful to consider long-term as well as short-term aspirations; strive to look about financial and job targets, including partnership ambitions, personal growth priorities, experiences you want to do, or skills you want to know. Draw up a timetable that tells when each element is to be achieved. Set SMART goals; realistic targets that are tangible, feasible, appropriate, and time-based. Break down big targets. For starters, you can set the aim of saving money and visiting other countries if you want to see the planet.

STICK TO THE UNDERTAKINGS.

To become successful, only planning is not enough; it is always necessary to hold the word and actions. When you think you're going to do it, do something. Likewise, don't tell someone if you don't know you can do something. Be frank about the boundaries. Should not cancel plans and seek not to cancel the same person twice. Make and stick to your commitments. Write down and put your obligations in places you can see. Be sure your efforts shift you towards your goals gradually. Check now and again, the priorities to guarantee that you step in the right direction.

BE EDUCATED.

Training and education allow you to reach your full ability through knowledge, expertise, and reputation. In terms of financial success, the more education you have (i.e., the higher you get), the more money you will probably make. In 2011, high-school students got a median weekly salary of $638, and those with bachelor's degrees earned $1053. During the same year, masters or students earned $1263 and $1551, respectively. Not all preparation must be standardized. Long-term jobs and apprenticeships are both beneficial ties to higher wages. A certificate can help increase your salary in your field. Skill yourself just for fun. The more you are aware of the world in which you work, the more doubts you have, and the more curious you are.

MANAGE YOUR FINANCES.

Learn how to handle your finances; irrespective of your income can help to ensure your financial security over time. Keep track of your expense. Subtract your monthly costs from your monthly revenue to calculate how much money you have per month available. Check your bank statements regularly to figure out where you are spending your money. This helps you avoid overpayments and ensures that your bank statements are correct. Understand your income. Be sure to consider the federal, state, and social security taxes deducted from your gross salary when calculating your income. Don't forget various deductions, such as health insurance premiums, savings bonds, and credit payments. The impact is your net income, which is what you take home. If you do not earn enough to cover your net costs, look at your expenses and see if you can change them. Save money. You need to invest some of your money into a savings account every month. Consider asking your employer to deposit part of your income directly into your savings account. Cautiously save. If your employer has a pension savings scheme, apply for your surplus money.

MANAGE YOUR TIME.

If essential tasks are discharged up to the last minute, they can cause unnecessary stress and increase the chance of error and neglect. Manage your time so you have sufficient time to complete your tasks effectively. Use a planner to keep you organized all day, week, and month. Place your mobile phone alerts and use the automatic tracker to handle your time better. Create a list of what you have to do on a given day and review each assignment when it is done. This allows you to be inspired and coordinated.

ENJOY THE MOMENT NOW.

When you focus on the past and think about future endlessly, you skip the current moment. Know that the past and the future are only fantasies, and there is real life here and now. Start paying attention to negative feelings and step on and enjoy the present moment. When a pessimistic thought pops into your mind, identify it, mark it negative thinking, and then let it dim. Daily meditation and mindfulness training will help to make you feel more normal. Get used to paying attention to the tiny things around you. Enjoy the warmth of the sun on your face, the sound of your feet walking on the ground, or your food in the restaurant at which you sit. Such stuff will allow you to stay quiet and enjoy every moment.

Don't equate your own life with the lives of others.

Unfortunately, many people evaluate their own success by contrasting it with other people. If you wish to be successful and happy, you must love your life for your own sake. Often people prefer to equate the low points of their own experience with the high aspects of the life of others. No matter how good a person's life looks, everyone is coping with traumatic incidents, depression, and other issues behind closed doors. Pay attention and restrict the use of social networks to remind you of this. Talk of all those who are poor, mentally sick, or in poverty, rather than comparing yourself with those who are "better off" than you are. This allows you to enjoy what you have rather than feel bad for yourself. Start volunteering to help make that more clear. It will also help to increase your satisfaction and confidence.

Count your blessings.

Whatever you do with your life, you will always be sad if you continually dwell on what you do not have. Instead, spend time appreciating the things you have every day. Think beyond material items, respect, and care about the good memories of your loved ones.

Look after your health.

Look after your family. A balanced body is essential for a healthy mind. Follow a healthy diet to make sure you don't have any supplements you lack. Talk to a doctor, nutritionist, and related healthcare providers to assess the cause of symptoms you might encounter, such as loss of strength or focus. Get plenty of workouts too, but pick your exercise as you want.

TRACK INCENTIVES.

Use it because you have a chance to shine. If you're afraid that you won't have the time and resources to have a decent shot, wonder: will that help my goals? If so, then drop other obligations to seek this chance. Note, only there are any opportunities. You can't deposit them. You do not throw out all your money or get rid of your safety net. It just means saying yes when you are given a step forward.

ENCIRCLE YOURSELF WITH OPTIMISTIC PEOPLE.

Make friends with people you admire for different reasons: because they are happy, kind, generous, successful at work, or otherwise prosperous. Join hands for those who have accomplished or are on their way to a shared target. Don't let envy get in the way: the success of no one is a challenge to you. When you make friends, ask yourself whether they make you feel inspired, optimistic, and comfortable, or lazy, frustrated, or incompetent. Choose to spend time with the good men, not those who derive motivation from you. If you have friends or family who regularly make you feel guilty, restricts the time you spend with them. Also, be sure to identify relationships that don't help you move towards your goals, stress yourself, or take too much time and energy without being reciprocal. Seek mentors of the people you admire. If you think anybody should help you, ask for your advice.

KNOW HOW EXPERTS ARE COMPETENT IN TRANSFORMING YOUR LIFE

You won't live long enough to imagine everything for yourself. And what a waste to try if you can learn from others who went before. Ben Franklin said in one of many great quotes, "Men either can buy their wisdom, or they can buy it from others. The big disappointment is that most consumers choose to purchase it and pay the full price for time and money. Your biggest aim in life and personal success should be to achieve the most significant possible number of them and then use them to help you do what you want to do and to become the person you want to become.

For instance:

You can follow a step by step process created by a best-selling author if you want to learn to write a book. Learn about your errors and benefit from your systems by following your book guide. In the end, it will save you time!

IMMEDIATE ACHIEVEMENT

You transform your life by completing only one essential goal; you create a blueprint for your subconscious mind's personal achievement. You will change your life and be automatically guided and driven to repeat that success in other things you try. This is the easiest way to bring order to your life. You will prepare yourself for success in other fields by facing obstacles and completing a significant goal in each area. In other words, you learn to excel. The more you do, the more you can accomplish. Each key to success, and particularly the first, builds your belief and confidence that next time you succeed, you achieve ultimate personal success. Seek to take advantage of your professional achievements in order to accomplish a goal in your profession or at college. You will finally establish a synergistic impact and realize that progress on both fronts is simpler.

CHAPTER 4
EFFECTIVE HABITS OF SUCCESSFUL PEOPLE

Ever wonder that it still feels like a challenge to get ahead? The fact is: if you want to excel immensely, you have to be incredibly disciplined. I have asked countless managers and entrepreneurs what they do every day to help them succeed, and they typically give credit for the simple everyday routines that have proven themselves over time. Most people question how they can be extremely successful and not know what they need to do to attain their desired results. Successful people are as they are because of their customs now. Habits determine 95% of the behavior of a person. What you are now and all you will ever do is contingent on the consistency of your habits. You will thrive and lead to a happy life by developing healthy behaviors and cultivating a productive approach. Here in this section, we are going to explain some habits of successful peoples.

THEY START THE DAY IN THE MORNING

One of the successful people 's core habits is to get out of bed early. It provides them with a sense of confidence to prepare items for their everyday activities. They use this opportunity by taking part in the rehearsal and preparation of the events during the day.

MEDITATION

Meditation has many physical and emotional effects, such as reducing stress, managing fear, increasing self-awareness, etc. Many people who excel in life have learned the untold benefits of meditation. They meditate every day as it strengthens their memory and gives several other advantages.

PEOPLE WHO EXCEL ARE ENDURING.

They know nothing to override determination and commitment, and they are accustomed never to pause until goals are met.

PRODUCTIVE PEOPLE ARE TRUSTING IN THEMSELVES.

Trust is the practice of improving oneself, knowledge, and talents. It is a process that builds unwavering self-confidence slowly but surely-an important element of success.

FOCUSED THINKING

Focused thinking is your mind's most alerted state because it allows your brain to concentrate best by removing all the distractions. For about 30 minutes, most productive individuals have a daily routine of reflecting on all important issues, such as wellbeing, connection, industry, etc. so they can properly evaluate it and create a proper plan for doing it.

GOOD PEOPLE BELIEVE HIGH.

You act big when you dream big, and tremendous things happen. What is the next big idea, project, enterprise about which you can think?

COMMITTED.

Their strong beliefs mean that they organize everything else in life around their key purpose and do everything it takes to make it happen.

SUCCESSFUL PEOPLE GENEROUSLY CONTRIBUTE.

Productive people are accustomed to interest in others. To succeed, seek ways to give and not get.

IT'S GOAL-ORIENTED

Successful people concentrate on targets. They are regular target setters and work with clear, written goals every day of their life, creating daily habits. These individuals are geared towards their goals. They know exactly what they want, they have it written down, they have written plans to do that, and revisit, and they work on their plans every day.

REGULAR WORKOUT

How can you succeed if you don't have a stress management plan? According to the United States Anxiety and Depression

Organization, 70 % of adults are depressed in the United States. That is one of the critical reasons that productive people get used to a routine workout because they know they can't do their best because they're under tension all the time.

They Are Powered by Tests

The success habit of highly productive people is motivated by performance. It consists of two activities. The first is the custom of continually studying in order to do more better what you do, and the second practice is the allocation of priorities. This means that you set very clear priorities on what you do and then focus on the most precious use of the time. Every productive person is deeply results-oriented.

Network with Other People

Successful people have a tremendous impact on their own success as they keep themself motivated. That is why effective people tend to build relationships with optimistic and inspired individuals in order to get the best individuals. They do their hardest to restrict their access to negative people because they feel it will negatively impact their personalities. They set a high standard for themselves

With respect to self-standard, everyone has the right to choose. However, successful people do not compromise themselves. They set a high bar for themselves as they are helping to generate a strong effort, determination, and performance that are important to progress.

Successful People Have Huge Willpower.

They have the power to see things without hesitation or decline. They let it happen as they like to. The biggest successes in the world are people who have shown the courage to keep their goals centered and constant.

PEOPLE WHO EXCEL HAVE COURAGE.

We recognize that there are mistakes and problems in all. Personally, having losses slows it down even further. Their practice of patience is not so much about waiting as to how to behave as they expect.

ACTION-ORIENTED

Successful people are geared towards practice. This exceptional skill they have is related to the constant operation. It is the most critical skill of project completion. It's the desire to get the job done fast. They are able to establish and sustain a sense of urgency and a passion for the practice. In whatever they do, a fast pace is important for their performance. They must resolve the delay, set their worries aside, and get 100% to reach the most significant goals. The combination of objective orientation, result orientation, and action orientation in itself will ensure virtually great success. I strongly recommend that you learn to use SMART goals to identify realistic targets that can be calculated and monitored.

TAKE ENOUGH SLEEP

Sufficient sleep is important to success in life. Not only does this sharpen your brain, but it also serves to improve your morale. Effective individuals know the value of enough sleep, and so they tend to sleep more every day that they can train for the best quality jobs.

DON'T DEPEND ON A SINGLE REVENUE SOURCE

Effective individuals often try to build several sources of income because they realize that they can not maintain financial security by relying solely on a single source of income. They usually have between three to five streams of income so that the economic downturn doesn't take too long.

THEY AVOID THE WASTE OF TIME

Time is money for a productive individual. They spend their days in experience because they realize that each day, they have a limited amount of time that they need to use wisely to excel. They tend to take advantage of opportunities that make them more successful instead of spending their time browsing Instagram, watching Netflix, etc.

EFFICIENT INDIVIDUALS ARE HOPEFUL.

Instead of fear, they choose positivity. Optimism is a perfect plan for a prosperous future – before they can stand forward and assume the initiative to do so, they will trust that the future will be great.

SUCCESSFUL INDIVIDUALS ARE FLEXIBLE.

They make it a routine of strength and adaptability. Many of them have succeeded in achieving anything different than what they first did. They know that the world always changes, and they refuse to lock themselves in a box.

PRODUCTIVE PEOPLE ARE MINDFUL OF THEIR "WHY."

Successful people are used to having an understanding of what they are doing. They have reflected on their motivations and intentions that in effect give them the confidence and the strength to proceed.

KEEP TRACK OF DAILY TASKS

It is important to get things done on time to succeed; that's why most successful people are used to having their activities record in a specific notebook or app to chart their day-to-day achievements. It allows them to keep in touch with all the relevant things they need to do.

CONTINUE THE DAY WITH SMALL SIGNIFICANT TASKS

One of the easiest ways to treat productive individuals is to rank them from small to big. When they continue their day and accomplish some of their essential activities, they get extra incentive and self-confidence to cope comfortably with other, bigger, and more challenging tasks.

THEY ARE CONSCIOUS OF HEALTH

Health awareness is the most important habit that highly successful people develop. So they keep an eye on their diet and only eat the best things in the right part. They must exercise regularly, continuously using all their body muscles and joints to keep it limber and fit. Finally, they will have strong rest and leisure habits, so that they can stay in a safe condition during their years in tandem with proper diet and exercise. Note, your wellbeing is the most precious thing you have, and it is entirely subject to your actions and the way you work.

THEY TREAT CHALLENGES AS GIFTS

Many people usually give up when they have problems because they are not able to deal with these problems. But successful people have a different story; for them, issues are like as an opportunity to improve and learn from these problems in the future.

THEY ACCEPT DEFEAT AND RESTART

Successful people never stay in the background because they have a new mindset. They try new stuff, make errors, and learn from it. That mentality is not healthy for many, as they are terrified of disappointment that prevents them from playing with new things.

STICK TO ROUTINE

It is not enough to establish a good everyday routine if you do not practice it. Not only do highly successful people invest time to develop these routines, but they also play an equal part in following these routines. They know that these rituals not only plan their lives but also save time and performance.

PAY ATTENTION TO INFORMATION

Paying attention to information will enhance things in terms of precision, time, and consistency. Many people ignore the details, which cost them time and money. Yet productive people prefer to pay careful attention to this consistency because they don't want to waste their valuable time and resources on a particular job again and again.

ARE HONEST

Honesty is the most critical behavior of successful people. In the end, the character you create while you live is more important than almost everything else. Honesty means that with everything you do, you follow the "principle of truth." For yourself and the world around you, you are utterly analytical. You give yourself simple principles and align yourself around your beliefs. You create a dream and live your life in line with the highest values. For someone or something, you never sacrifice your dignity or peace of mind. This integrity is necessary for your enjoyment of all the other positive habits you create.

SELF-DISCIPLINED.

One more habit of successful people is self-discipline and the only habit that ensures the others.

Your ability to manage, master yourself, and control yourself is the fundamental attribute that will help you to grow as an individual. The practice of self-discipline correlates with achievement in all areas of life. If you want some support when moving to the life of your dreams, you can check out the encouraging achievement quotations.

Any of these patterns can be formed with goals, outcomes, action-oriented, people-oriented, health-conscious, truthful, and self-disciplined performance. You are where you are now, regardless of your habits and what you are doing. Your routines have grown, mostly by chance, since you were a kid. You will now take complete charge over the shaping over your personality and character, and everything that happens to you in your future, by choosing to decide your behaviors at present, which will lead you to high achievement.

And you will enjoy sharing success if you build the same positive habits of other productive people.

EXERCISE SELF-CONTROL

Self-control has the potential to boost concentration and decision-making. It has an immense effect on the success that successful people learn. Most of them are trying to spend some time on issues that are tenting, which do not make a significant difference in their performance. That's because it makes the entire self-stress-free cycle for them.

ALWAYS LOOKING FOR A SOLUTION

Many people are accustomed to complaining and to suggest frivolous excuses if they can not get what they want. Even for productive men, the story is unique. They try tirelessly to find the best answer, also though it seems complicated for some.

CONCLUSION

There is no measure of success and certainly no answer to how to succeed in life. But by looking at certain successful people's habits, you can learn new tactics and strategies in your own daily lives. Grow up and develop these abilities, and you can find yourself more capable of meeting your goals and achieving your desired life achievement over time. You have to be successful.

I may list one million more tips on how to excel in life, but if you are unable to do the work, it won't be worth it.

To become successful, you need to learn a few skills and habits which is summarized as,

- Fear of failure: You need to learn how to overcome business fear.
- How to Explore the Globe?
- You need to explore How you can work for yourself?

Although all of these looks difficult initially, it will help you get into the right mood and the right mindset.